Last Supper Maze

Can you help the disciples find the right house to set up for the
Passover meal in Jerusalem? (You can read this story in Matthew 26 verses 17-19.)

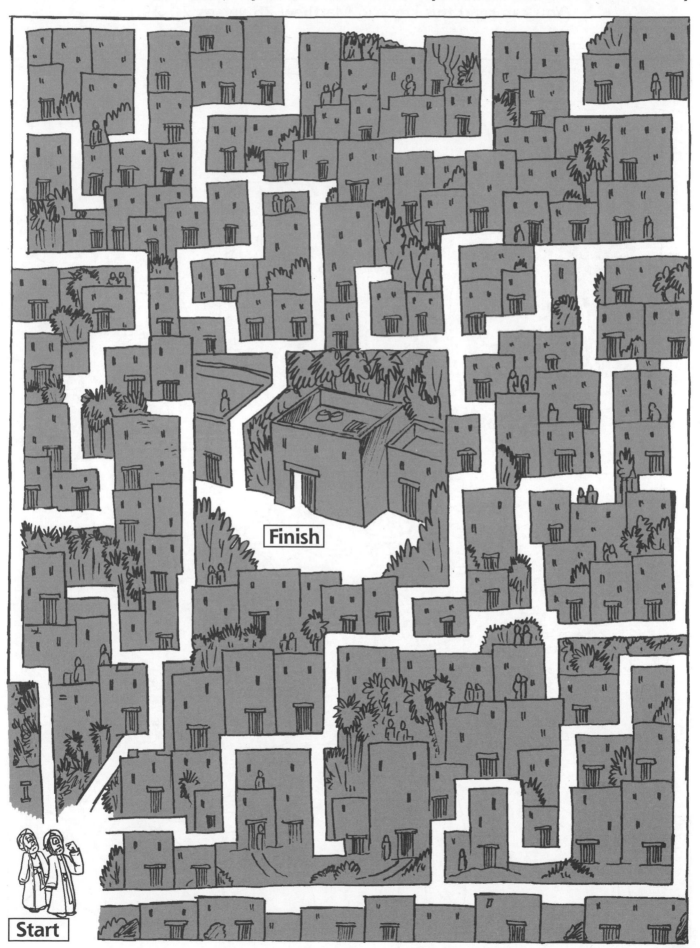

Finish

Start

Colouring Sheet

Here's a picture of Jesus and His disciples enjoying the Last Supper together.
Can you see Jesus breaking the bread?
(You can read this story in Matthew 26 verses 20-29.)

Garden Maze

Can you help the disciples find Jesus in the Garden of Gethsemane?
(You can read this story in Matthew 26 verses 36-38.)

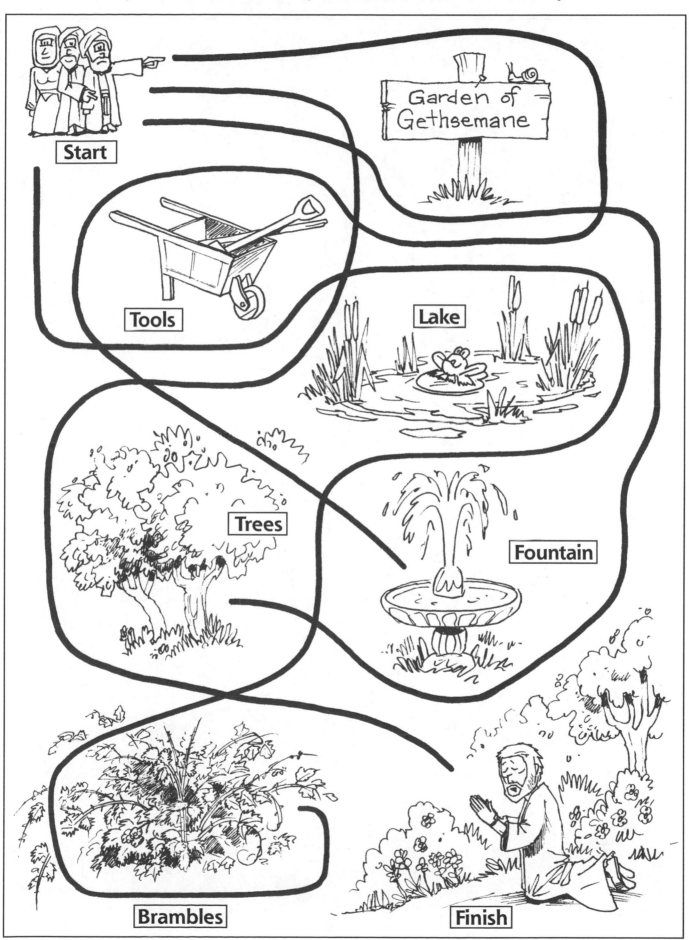

Start

Garden of Gethsemane

Tools

Lake

Trees

Fountain

Brambles

Finish

Spot The Difference

Can you spot the 10 differences between these 2 pictures of Jesus & the disciples in the garden of Gethsemane? (You can read this story in Matthew 26 verses 47-56.)

The Easter Story: The Garden of Gethsemane

Look-And-Find

See if you can you find:

A dog

A frog

A snake in a tree

A woman hanging out washing

2 lizards on 2 walls

A cockerel crowing

A child eating, sitting on a box

A carpet with a spot on it

2 spears leaning against a wall

Easter Wordsearch

Can you find these words in the letter grid below? Words can be spelt up and down, forwards and backwards, or diagonally! Letters can be used in more than one word too! Once you have crossed off all the letters in the word grid, you will find that the first 13 remaining letters in the grid spell out a message for you. Write it in the spaces below:

_ _ _ _ _   _ _ _ _ _   _ _ _

ALIVE	EASTER	KING	SIMON
ANGEL	GETHSEMANE	LORD	SOLDIERS
BARABBAS	GOLGOTHA	MARY	SUNDAY
BREAD	HEAVEN	PETER	SUPPER
CROWN	HEROD	PILATE	TEMPLE
CROSS	JERUSALEM	PRIEST	TOMB
DARKNESS	JESUS	ROMAN	WINE
DISCIPLE	JUDAS	SILVER	WITNESS

S	A	D	U	J	J	E	S	Y	A	P	E	T	E	R
R	O	M	A	N	U	S	L	A	H	S	I	M	O	N
S	S	E	N	K	R	A	D	D	T	O	A	G	T	V
S	O	L	D	I	E	R	S	N	O	S	L	N	O	E
R	E	P	P	U	S	S	Y	U	G	A	I	I	M	O
A	N	G	E	L	U	J	I	S	L	B	V	K	B	H
J	E	R	U	S	A	L	E	M	O	B	E	N	I	W
E	N	A	M	E	S	H	T	E	G	A	P	Y	X	E
T	E	L	P	I	C	S	I	D	D	R	I	C	A	P
S	S	E	N	T	I	W	P	H	I	A	N	S	I	T
S	I	N	S	H	E	A	V	E	N	B	T	L	E	C
D	C	L	O	R	D	E	S	R	S	E	A	M	R	S
F	O	P	V	F	H	T	V	O	R	T	P	O	J	E
U	N	D	A	E	R	B	F	D	E	L	S	I	L	B
M	A	R	Y	C	R	O	W	N	E	S	U	S	E	J

Copy And Colour

Copy the picture of the trial of Jesus by drawing the contents of each square in turn into the blank grid below. Then you can colour your picture in.
(You can read this story in Matthew 27 verses 11-26.)

Dot-To-Dot

Can you join the dots to reveal the picture of what Peter saw when he denied Jesus?
(You can read this story in Mark 14 verses 66-72.)

Start Here

Cross Maze

Can you find your way through the Cross Maze to the finish?

Finish

Start

(You can read this story in Luke 24 verses 36-43.)

Colouring Sheet

Here's a picture for you to colour in, of Jesus carrying the cross through the streets of Jerusalem. Can you see the mice watching from the box? (You can read this story in John 19 verses 17-19.)

Easter Crossword

ACROSS

3 Ruler of a kingdom.

7 Name of the hill, outside Jerusalem where Jesus was crucified, starts with "Gol" (see Matthew 27:33)

8 A special messenger from heaven, seen at Jesus' tomb.

11 Place where Jesus went after he came back to life, starts with "H".

12 Opposite of lightness, which happened when Jesus was crucified.

13 The first name of the man who betrayed Jesus, _ _ _ _ _ Iscariot.

14 Wooden object that Jesus was nailed to.

16 Food broken by Jesus at the Last Supper.

17 Another name for a grave, starts with the letter "T".

19 Day after Saturday.

20 Name of the king in Jerusalem. (see Luke 23:8)

DOWN

1 Name of one of Jesus' disciples, also called Peter.

2 Second name of the Roman governor, Pontius P _ _ _ _ _

4 Drink of the Last Supper.

5 Precious metal used to make coins, starts with the letter "S".

6 People in an army, who took Jesus to be crucified, Roman... starts with "Sol".

9 _ _ _ _ _ the Christ, or The Messiah.

10 Day we celebrate Jesus coming back to life.

14 _ _ _ _ _ of Thorns, put on Jesus head by the Roman soldiers.

15 Name of the mother of Jesus.

18 Name of the last evening meal Jesus shared with his followers, the Last...

Mary Dot-To-Dot

Join the dots to reveal the scene of what happened after Jesus died on the cross.
(You can read this story in John 20 verses 15-18.)

Colouring Sheet

Colour in the picture. There are two angels in the tomb where his body
was placed and you can see Mary Magdalene kneeling in front of Jesus.
(You can read this story in Luke 24 verses 1-8.)

Spot The Tomb

All the pictures below are in pairs, except one - can you spot it?

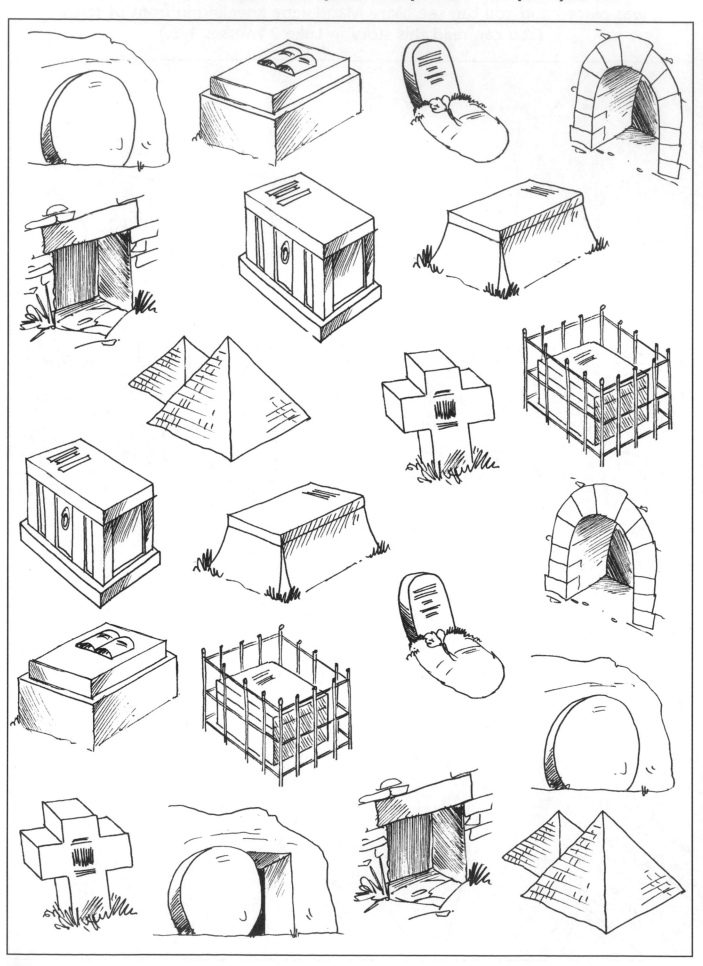

Alpha-Words

Some letters of the alphabet are missing from the squares below.
Can you use the missing letters to find...

1) A food that Jesus broke at the last supper?

2) The name of an animal that people can ride?

3) The name of a messenger from heaven, sent from God, seen at the tomb of Jesus?

Gospel Maze

Can you help the disciples find their way through the maze,
and help them spread the Good News that Jesus is alive?
(You can read this story in Matthew 28 verses 16-20.)

Colouring Sheet

Colour in the picture of Jesus going up into heaven.
(You can read this story in Luke 24 verses 50-53.)

Easter is a very special time...

It's when we remember how much God loves us.

The Bible says that we have all done things that are wrong and have lived as though we were the boss of our lives – the Bible calls this sin. When we live like this it hurts God because He made us and everything in the world. He is the boss. We cannot be friends with him because of our sin and deserve to be punished. This is really sad.

The great news is that God loves us and wants to be friends with us again. So God did something really special. He gave us a gift – His Son, Jesus. At Easter we remember Jesus' special journey. He went to the city of Jerusalem where Roman soldiers crucified Him. This was a horrible thing to do. Remember, Jesus had never done anything wrong.

But it was all part of God's big plan. Jesus died so that we could be forgiven. He was buried in a cave and stayed there for three days. His followers were very sad.

But Jesus is God and He couldn't stay dead. Jesus rose again! He is alive – never to die again!

Because Jesus died on a cross for us, all those who are truly sorry for their sin and ask Jesus to be the boss of their lives can be forgiven and live with Him forever! This is the great story of Easter.

Answers...

Spot The Difference (p4)

Look-And-Find (p5)

Easter Wordsearch (p6)
Message: JESUS LOVES YOU

Cross Maze (p9)

Easter Crossword (p13)

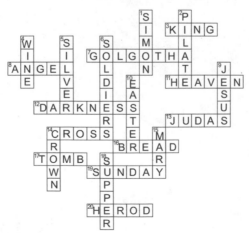

Spot The Tomb (p16)

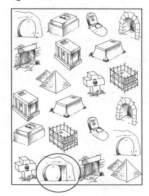

Alpha-Words (p17)

1) BREAD
2) DONKEY
3) ANGEL

Published by 10Publishing, a division of 10ofThose Limited. ISBN: 9781906173449.
Written and illustrated by Martin Young. Typeset by Diane Warnes. Printed in the UK.
10Publishing, Unit C, Tomlinson Road, Leyland, PR25 2DY, England. Email: info@10ofthose.com. Website: www.10ofthose.com